The Book of Good MANNERS

If thou never saw'st good manners, then thy manners must be wicked. Touchstone

By

Philip Dormer Stanhope

Fourth Earl of Chesterfield

and the editors of Bellerophon Books

Young King Louis XV is on the front cover.

Manner

I here list those necessary ornamental accomplishments (without which, no one living can either please or rise in the world) which only require your care and attention to possess.

To speak elegantly; without which nobody will hear you with patience, and, consequently, you will speak to very little purpose.

An agreeable and distinct elocution, without which nobody will hear you with patience. You need take much less pains for it than Demosthenes did.

A distinguished politeness of manners and address; which common sense, observation, good company, and imitation will infallibly give you, if you will accept it.

A genteel carriage, and graceful motions, with a fashionable air.

To be extremely clean in your person, and perfectly well dressed, according to the fashion, be that what it will.

Upon the whole, take it for granted, that without these accomplishments, all you know, and all you can do, will avail you very little.

When you see a person, who is universally allowed to shine as an agreeable well-bred person, pay attention to him, or to her, watch him, or her, carefully. You will find that they take care never to say or do anything that can be construed into a slight, or a negligence; or that can, in any degree, mortify people's vanity and self-love; on the contrary, you will notice that they make people pleased with them by making them first pleased with themselves; they show respect, regard, esteem, and attention; they sow them with care, and they reap them in plenty.

These amiable accomplishments are all to be acquired by use and imitation, for we are, in truth, more than half what we are, by imitation. The great point is, *to choose good models*, and to study them with care. People unconsciously imitate not only the air, the manners, and the vices, of those with whom they commonly converse, but their virtues too, and even their way of thinking. Persist, therefore, in keeping the best company, and

3

you will, without realizing it, become like them; if you add attention and observation, you will very soon be one of them.

There is infinite utility and advantage in presenting yourself with coolness and unconcern in any and every company. One who has no experience of the world is inflamed with anger, or annihilated with shame, at every disagreeable incident. A worldly person seems not to understand what cannot or ought not be resented. If the worldly person makes a slip, he, or she, recovers it by coolness, instead of plunging deeper by confusion, like a stumbling horse. Unworldly people have babbling countenances, and are unskillful enough to show, what they have sense enough not to tell. In the course of the world, one must very often put on an easy, frank countenance, upon very disagreeable occasions;

one must seem pleased, when very much otherwise; one must be able to accost and receive with smiles, those whom one would much rather meet with swords. One must not turn him—or her—self inside out. All this may, nay must be done without falsehood and treachery. Good manners are necessary guards of the decency and peace of society.

This is about the *duty*, the *utility*, and the *means* of pleasing — that is of being what the French call *aimable*. Whoever is not *aimable*, is in truth, *nobody at all*. Those who are amiable will make almost as many friends as they do acquaintances. Civility is the essential article towards pleasing, and is the result of good nature and of good sense; but good breeding is the decoration, and only to be acquired by a minute attention to, and experience of, good company. In good breeding, the *manner* always adorns and dignifies the *matter*.

The manner is often as important as the matter, sometimes more so; a favor may make an enemy, and an injury may make a friend, according to the different manner in which they are done. Gentleness of manner with firmness of mind is a short but full description of human perfection.

Manner is all in everything; it is by manner only that you can please, and consequently rise.

The Importance of Pleasing

It is not sufficient to deserve well, one must please well too.

You must be sensible that you cannot rise in the world without forming connections and persuading different characters to conspire on your point. You must make them your dependents without their knowing it and dictate to them while you seem to be directed by them These necessary connections can only be formed or preserved by an uninterrupted series of attentions, politeness and some constraint. You must engage their hearts if you would have their support. If you expect to receive strength from them, they must receive either pleasure or

advantage from you. Strong minds have undoubtedly an advantage over weak ones, but their advantage is to be gained by degrees, and by those arts which experience of the world teaches; for few people are mean enough to be bullied, though most are weak enough to be bubbled.

To please people is a great step toward persuading them. Men and women are oftener led by their hearts than by their understandings. The way to their hearts is through their senses; please their eyes and their ears and the work is half done. A look, a gesture, an attitude, a tone of voice all bear their parts in the great work of pleasing.

The art of pleasing is a very necessary one to possess, but a very difficult one to acquire. It can hardly be reduced to rules; and your own good sense and observation will teach you more of it than I can. "Do as you would be done by," is the surest method that I know of pleasing.

It is an active, cheerful, obliging, attractive good-breeding that must gain you the good-will of men and the affections of women. You must carefully watch and attend to their passions, their tastes, their little humors and weaknesses. For instance, suppose you invited anybody to dine with you, you ought to recollect if he had any favorite dish and take care to provide it for him and when it came, you should say, "You seemed to prefer this dish, so I ordered it. This is the wine I thought you liked and therefore I obtained some." The more trifling these things are the more they prove your attention for the person and are the more engaging.

If you will please people, you must please them in their own way; and, as you cannot make them what they should be, you

must take them as they are. We are complicated machines; and, though we have one main-spring that gives motion to the whole, we have an infinity of little wheels, which, in their turns, retard, precipitate and sometimes stop the motion. Seek first, then, for

the predominant passion of the character you mean to win and influence and address yourself to it, but don't forget the lesser passions. There are many avenues to everyone, and when you cannot get at them through the great one, try the roundabout way and you will arrive at last.

In the course of the world, the qualifications of the chameleon are often necessary; nay, they must be carried a little farther and exerted a little sooner, for you should, to a certain degree, take the hue of the person you want to be on good terms with.

There is nothing that people bear more impatiently or forgive less than contempt; an injury is much sooner forgotten than an insult. If, therefore, you would rather please than offend, remember to have that constant attention which flatters everyone's little vanity. People have various objects in which they may excel, and though they love to hear justice done to them where they know that they excel, yet they are most and best flattered upon those points where they wish to excel and yet are doubtful whether they do or not.

Remember that to please is almost to prevail, or at least a necessary previous step to it. You, who have your fortune to make, should most particularly study this art.

People

If you want to gain the affection and friendship of particular people, try to find out their main excellence, if they have one, and their prevailing weakness, which everybody has; and do justice to the one, and more than justice to the other. You will easily discover every one's prevailing vanity by observing his favorite topic of conversation; for everyone talks most of what he has most a mind to be thought to excel in. Touch him but there, and you touch him to the quick.

Almost all people are born with all the passions, to a certain degree; but almost everyone has a prevailing one, to which the others are subordinate. Search everyone for that ruling passion; pry into the recesses of his heart, and observe the different workings of the same passion in different people. And when you have found out the prevailing passion of anyone, remember never to trust him where that passion is concerned. Work upon him by it, if you please; but be upon your guard yourself against it, whatever he may say to you.

I recommend to you an innocent piece of art: flattering people behind their backs, in the presence of those who will not fail to repeat and even amplify the praise to the party concerned. This is, of all flattery, the most pleasing and, consequently, the most effectual.

Behave prudently towards those whom you do not like. The person who can command his temper and countenance the best will always have an infinite advantage over the other. One must often yield, in order to prevail; one must humble oneself to be exalted; one must be all things to all men to gain some.

Let your enemies be disarmed by the gentleness of your manner, but let them feel at the same time the steadiness of your just resentment; for there is a great difference between bearing malice, which is always ungenerous, and a resolute self-defense, which is always prudent and justifiable.

Never yield to that temptation, which to most young people is very strong, of exposing other people's weaknesses for the sake of showing your own superiority. You may get the laugh for the present, but you will make enemies by it forever. The more you know, the more modest you should be: that modesty is the

sweetest way of gratifying your vanity. Even where you are sure, seem rather doubtful; represent but do not pronounce; and, if you would convince others, seem open to conviction yourself.

Take care never to seem dark and mysterious; if you seem mysterious with others, they will be really so with you and you will know nothing. Have a real reserve with almost everybody and have a seeming reserve with almost nobody; for it is very disagreeable to seem reserved and very dangerous not to be so.

Grace and Good-Breeding

All rational beings (I take it for granted) propose to themselves some object more important than mere breathing and obscure animal existence. They desire to distinguish themselves among their fellow creatures. In this, any one of common sense may, by common application, be sure to excel. And it is essential to your interest, by your own good-breeding, to secure the interest of others to yours. You must adorn yourself with all those graces and accomplishments which, without *solidity*, are frivolous; but, without which, solidity is, to a great degree, useless. As learning, honor and virtue are absolutely necessary to gain you the esteem and admiration of mankind, politeness and good-breeding are equally necessary to make you welcome and agreeable in conversation and common life. It is good-breeding alone that can influence people in your favor at first sight, more time being necessary to discover greater talents. This good-breeding, you know does not consist in bows and formal ceremony, but in an easy, civil and respectful behavior.

Air, address, manners and graces are of infinite advantage to whoever has them. The scholar without good-breeding is a pedant; the philosopher a cynic; the soldier a brute; and everyone disagreeable. Examine why such and such people please and delight you more than such and such others of equal merit, and you will always find that it is because the former have the graces and the latter do not. Awkwardness of carriage is very alienating, and a total negligence of dress and air is an impertinent insult to custom and fashion. Awkwardness and ill-breeding shock me to that degree that, where I meet with them, I cannot find in my heart to inquire into the intrinsic merit of that person; I hastily decide in myself that he can have none. If you have not a graceful address, liberal and engaging manners, a prepossessing air and a good degree of eloquence, you will be nothing; but will have the daily mortification of seeing people with not one-tenth of your merit or knowledge get the start of you and disgrace you both in company and in business.

Good-breeding is not the showish trifle which some people think it; it is a solid good; it prevents a great deal of mischief; creates, adorns, and strengthens friendships; keeps hatred within bounds; and promotes good-humor and good-will in families, where the want of gentleness is commonly the cause of discord. Civility is the essential article toward pleasing and is the result of good-nature and good-sense; but good-breeding is the decoration, the lustre of civility, and only to be acquired by a minute attention to and experience of good company.

The characteristic of well-bred persons is to converse with their inferiors without insolence and with their superiors with respect and with ease. They converse with equals, whether acquainted with them or not, upon common topics, that are not, however, quite frivolous, without the least concern of mind or awkwardness of body.

Next to graceful speaking, a genteel carriage and a graceful manner of presenting yourself are extremely necessary. Engaging manners, a distinguished politeness, an almost irresistable address, a superior gracefulness in all you say and do: it is this alone that can give all your other talents their full value and lustre. One who will take care always to be in the right in these things may afford to be sometimes a little in the wrong in more essential things. Whatever pleases you most in others will without fail please others in you. Take it for granted, the best-bred people

will always be the best received wherever they go. There is no occasion in the world in which brusqueness is becoming. Whatever one ought to do is to be done with ease and unconcern; whatever is improper must not be done at all.

Nothing sinks people into low company so surely as timidity and diffidence. If they think that they shall not, you may depend upon it, they will not please. A diamond while rough has indeed its intrinsic value; but, till polished, is of no use and would be neither sought for nor worn. Its great lustre proceeds from its solidity and strong cohesion of parts; but, without the last polish, it would remain forever a dirty rough mineral.

— Upon the whole, I do desire, and insist, that, from after dinner til you go to bed, you make good-breeding, address and manners, your serious object and your only care. Without them, you will be nobody; with them, you may be anything.

Speaking and Conversation

Cicero says very truly that it is glorious to excel other people in that very article in which people excel brutes, speech.

It is a great advantage for anyone to be able to talk neither ignorantly nor absurdly upon any subject. Most people have ears, but few have judgment; tickle those ears and you will catch their judgments, such as they are. To be heard with success, you must be heard with pleasure: words are the dress of thoughts, which should no more be presented in rags, tatters and dirts than your person should. I should prefer moderate matter, adorned with all the beauties and elegances of style, to the strongest matter in the world ill-worded and ill-delivered.

I have frequently known a person's fortune decided for ever by his first address; and no one can make a fortune or reputation without speaking well. If you will persuade you must first please; and if you will please you must tune your voice to harmony, you must articulate every syllable distinctly, your emphases and cadences must be strongly and properly marked; and the whole together must be graceful and engaging; if you do not speak in that manner, you had much better not speak at all.

It is not enough to speak the language in its utmost purity and according to the rules of grammar, but you must speak it elegantly, use the best and most expressive words and put them in the best order. You should likewise adorn what you say by proper metaphors, similes and other figures of speech; and enliven it by quick and sprightly turns of wit. Deliver and pronounce what you say gracefully and distinctly. Consult your own ear to avoid cacophony and, what is near as bad, monotony.

Think also of your gesture and looks, when you are speaking even upon the most trifling subjects. The same things differently expressed, looked, and delivered, cease to be the same things. I repeat it, and repeat it again, and shall never cease repeating it to you, air, manners, graces, style, elegancy, and all those ornaments, must now be the objects of your attention; it is now or never, that you must acquire them. You have not one moment to lose.

17

Always look people in the face when you speak with them; not doing it is thought to imply conscious guilt; besides that, you lose the advantage of observing by their countenances what impression your discourse makes upon them.

Talk often, but not long; in that case, if you do not please, at least you are sure not to tire your hearers.

Tell stories very seldom and never but when they are very apt and very short. Frequent recourse to narrative betrays great want of imagination.

Neither repeat nor receive scandal willingly; as in robbery, the receiver is always thought as bad as the thief.

Mimicry, which is the common and favorite amusement of little low minds, is in utmost contempt with great ones. The person mimicked is insulted; and an insult is never forgiven.

18

Let your manner, your air, your terms and your tone of voice be soft and gentle and that easily and naturally, not affectedly. Use palliatives when you contradict, such as, "I may be mistaken," "I am not sure, but I believe," "I should think," etc. Finish any argument with some little good-humoured pleasantry, to show that you are neither hurt yourself, nor meant to hurt your antagonist.

Appear to have rather less wit than you really have. A wise person will live as much within his wit as his income. You may be admired for your wit, but nothing but good sense and qualities can make you loved. They are substantial everyday wear. Wit is for holidays, where people go chiefly to be stared at.

You must ever take care that the given subject of conversation does not lead you into any impropriety. In mixed companies, different ages and sexes are to be differently addressed. You

19

would not talk of your pleasures to people of a certain age, gravity, and dignity; they justly expect from young people a degree of deference and regard. You should be full as easy with them as with people of your own years; but your manner must be different; more respect must be implied; and it is not amiss to insinuate, that from them you expect to learn. Do not run your own present humor and disposition indiscriminately against everybody; but observe, conform to, and adopt theirs.

Constant experience has shown me, that great purity and elegance of style, with a graceful elocution, cover a multitude of faults, in either a speaker or a writer. Gain the heart, or you gain nothing; the eyes and the ears are the only roads to the heart. Merit and knowledge will not gain hearts, though they will secure them when gained. Engage the eyes by your address, air, and motions; soothe the ears, by the elegancy and harmony of your diction; the heart will certainly follow, and the whole man or woman will as certainly follow the heart. I must repeat it to you, over and over again, that, with all the knowledge which you may have at present, or hereafter acquire, and with all the merit that

ever man had, if you have not a graceful address, liberal and engaging manners, a prepossessing air, and a good degree of eloquence in speaking and writing, you will be nobody.

Of all things, banish egotism out of your conversation and never think of entertaining people with your own personal concerns or private affairs; though they are interesting to you, they are tedious and impertinent to everybody else; besides that, one cannot keep one's own private affairs too secret.

Air, looks, gestures, graces, enunciation, proper accents, just emphasis, speaking and tuneful cadences, are full as necessary as the matter itself. Make yourself a pure English style; it requires nothing but application. And after, at least, if not before you have said a thing, reflect if you could not have said it better. There is no one occasion in the world, in which a brusque tone is becoming.

I should be outrageous if I heard you mutter your words unintelligibly, stammer in your speech, or hesitate, misplace, and mistake in your narrations. Court the Graces all your life.

21

Dress and Appearance

A pleasing figure is a perpetual letter of recommendation.

Dress is an article not to be neglected, and I hope you do not neglect it; it helps in the first round, which is often decisive. By dress I mean your clothes being well made, fitting you, in the fashion and not above it; your hair well done, and a general cleanliness and spruceness in your person. Neglect nothing.

Dress is a very foolish thing; and yet it is a very foolish thing for someone not to be well dressed according to his way of life.

The difference between a man of sense and a fop, is that a fop values himself upon his dress; and a man of sense laughs at it but at the same time he knows he must not neglect it.

Adorning your person is not only not ridiculous, but proper and becoming. Negligence would imply, either an indifference about pleasing, or else an insolent security of pleasing, without using those means to which others are obliged to have recourse. When I was your age, I desired to shine, as far as I was able, in every part of life. A young person should be ambitious to shine in everything. Showing and shining people always get the better of all others.

It is by being well dressed, not finely dressed, that one should be distinguished. Take care always to be dressed like the reasonable people of your own age, in the place where you are; whose dress is never spoken of one way or another, as either too negligent or too studied.

There are those disagreeable tricks and awkwardnesses which many people contract when they are young, by the negligence of their parents, and cannot get quit of them when they are old, such as odd motions, postures, and ungenteel carriage. But there is likewise an awkwardness of the mind, that ought to be, and with care may be, avoided: as, for instance, to mistake or forget names; to speak of Mr. What-d'you-call-him, or Mrs. Thingum or How-d'you-call-her, is excessively awkward and ordinary. Attention and civility please all those to whom they are paid; you will please others in proportion as you are attentive and civil to them.

Are you sufficiently upon your guard against awkward

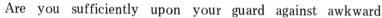

attitudes, and ill-bred, and disgusting habits, such as scratching yourself, putting your fingers in your mouth, nose, and ears, and other tricks acquired at school, often neglected afterwards?

I insist that you wash your teeth the first thing that you do every morning, for four or five minutes, and wash your mouth five or six times ... Nothing looks more ordinary, vulgar, and illiberal, than dirty hands, and ugly, uneven and ragged nails. I do not suspect you of that shocking, awkward trick of biting yours; but that is not enough; you must keep the ends of them smooth and clean.

Style is the dress of thoughts; and let them be ever so just, if your style is homely, coarse, and vulgar, they will appear to much disadvantage, and be as ill received as your person, though ever so well proportioned, would, if dressed in rags, dirt, and tatters.

Pleasure

Pleasure is the rock which most young people split upon; they launch out with crowded sails in quest of it, but without a compass to direct their course or reason sufficient to steer the vessel; for want of which, pain and shame, instead of pleasure, are the returns of their voyage.

How to sail his bicycle,
And how to wheel his boat,
Were questions that perplexed the mind
Of Sportive Dicky Sloat.

At last he worked the problem out
With secret toil and fuss,
And anxious friends were pleased to see
He solved the question —

—Thus.

Choose your pleasures for yourself and do not let them be imposed upon you. Follow nature and not fashion; weigh the present enjoyment of your pleasures against the necessary consequences of them, and then let your own common sense determine your choice. Pleasure is necessarily reciprocal; no one feels it who does not at the same time give it. To be pleased, one must please. The pleasures that you would feel, you must earn; people who give themselves up to all, feel none sensibly.

Real people of fashion and pleasure observe decency; at least they neither borrow nor affect vices.

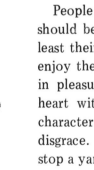

People of pleasure, though not always so scrupulous as they should be, and as one day they will wish they had been, refine at least their pleasures by taste, accompany them with decency and enjoy them with dignity. There is a certain dignity to be kept up in pleasure as well as in business. In love, you may lose your heart with dignity; but if you lose your nose, you lose your character in the bargain. Every pleasure has its neighboring disgrace. Mark carefully the line that separates them and rather stop a yard short than step an inch beyond it.

27

You must take part in pleasures in order to learn the manners of good company. In premeditated or formal business, people conceal or at least endeavour to conceal their characters; whereas

pleasures discover them and the heart breaks out through the guard of the understanding. These are often propitious moments to improve.

Divide your time between useful occupations and elegant pleasures. The morning belongs to study, business and serious conversation. From sitting down to dinner, the proper business of the day is pleasure, unless real business, which must never be postponed for pleasure, happens accidentally to interfere. Pleasure must not be the business of a person of sense and character; but it may be, and is, his relief, his reward. An uninterrupted life of pleasure is as insipid as it is contemptible. Some hours given every day to serious business must whet both the mind and the senses to enjoy those of pleasure.

— It is not only reasonable, but useful too, that your evenings should be devoted to amusements and pleasures; and therefore I not only allow but recommend, that they should be spent at gatherings, balls, theatre, and in the best companies; with this restriction only, that the consequences of the evenings' diversions may not break in upon the mornings' studies.

Take warning, and enjoy every moment; pleasures do not commonly last so long as life, and therefore should not be neglected; and the longest life is too short for knowledge, consequently every moment is precious.

Virtues and Vices

Every excellence and virtue has its kindred vice or weakness; and, if carried beyond certain bounds, sinks into the one or the other. Generosity often runs into profusion, economy into avarice, courage into rashness, caution into timidity, and so on. I believe there is more judgment required for the conduct of our virtues than for avoiding their opposite vices. Vice is so deformed that it shocks us at first sight, and would hardly ever attract us if it did not at first wear the mask of some virtue. But virtue is so beautiful that it charms us at first sight, engages us more and more upon further acquaintance and we think excess impossible. It is here that judgment is necessary, to moderate and direct the effects of an excellent cause.

There is nothing so delicate as your moral character and nothing which it is in your interest so much to preserve pure. Should

you be suspected of injustice, malignity, perfidy, lying, etc., all the parts and knowledge in the world will never procure you esteem, friendship or respect. Without this purity, you can have no dignity of character; and without dignity of character, it is impossible to rise in the world. You must be respectable if you will be respected.

A light trifling way of declining invitations to vice and folly is more effectual than grave philosophical refusals.

I will hope that you have no vices; but if, unfortunately, you should have any, at least I beg of you to be content with your own and to adopt nobody other's. The adoption of vice has

ruined ten times more young people than natural inclinations. People easily pardon in the young the common irregularities of the senses; but they do not forgive the least vice of the heart. The heart never grows better by age; I fear rather worse, always harder. A young liar will be an old one and a young knave will only be a greater knave as he grows older.

Never be ashamed of doing what is right. You know what virtue is; you may have it if you will; it is in everyone's power; and miserable the person who has it not. Just give me virtuous actions and I will not quibble about the motives.

Good and Bad Company

A young person is generally judged of by the company he keeps — and it is a very fair way of judging; and though you will not at first be able to make your way perhaps, into the best company, it is always in your power to avoid bad.

To keep good company, especially at your first setting out, is the way to receive good impressions. People are, in general, what they are made, by education and company, from fifteen to twenty-five. Lay aside the best book whenever you can go into the best company; and, depend upon it, you change for the better. Awkwardness can proceed but from two causes: not having kept good company or not having attended to it.

Good company is not what respective sets of company are pleased either to call or think themselves, but is that company which all the people of the place call and acknowledge to be

good company. It consists chiefly of people of rank and character, and people distinguished by particular merit or eminency in liberal art or science. Many people without merit intrude into it by their own forwardness, and others slide into it by the protection of some considerable person. But, in the main, the good predominates, and people of infamous and blasted characters are never admitted. In this fashionable good company, the best manners and the best language are most unquestionably to be learned.

Endeavour, as much as you can, to keep company with people above you. There you rise, as much as you sink with people below you; for you are whatever the company you keep is. Do not, when I say company above you, think that I mean with regard to their birth; that is the least consideration: I mean with regard to their merit, and the light in which the world considers them.

Bad company is, whatever is not generally allowed to be good company; it will be impossible for you, in the common course of life, not to fall sometimes into bad company; but get out of it as soon and as well as you can. There are some companies so blasted and scandalous, that to have been with them twice would hurt your character. *Low* company, which young people, at their first appearance in the world, are too apt to like, from a degree of bashfulness and laziness, is indeed not easily rubbed off. If you sink into this sort of company but for one year you will never emerge from it, but remain as obscure and insignificant as they are themselves. I mean, by low company insignificant people, distinguished by no one particular merit or talent, unless, perhaps, by soaking and sotting out their evenings; for drinking is generally the dull occupation of such company.

You may ask me, whether people have it always in their power to get into the best company? and how? Yes, they have, by deserving it. Merit and good-breeding will make their way, everywhere. Knowledge will introduce them, and good-breeding will endear them to the best companies. You will find, in every company, two principal figures, the fine lady and the fine gentleman, who absolutely give the law of wit, language, fashion and taste to the rest of that society. With a moderate share of sagacity, you will, before you have been half an hour in their company, easily discover these two principal figures; both by the deference which you will observe the whole company pay them, and by that easy, careless, and serene air, which their conscious-

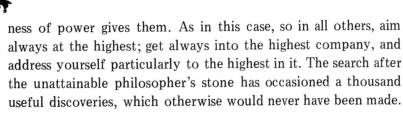

ness of power gives them. As in this case, so in all others, aim always at the highest; get always into the highest company, and address yourself particularly to the highest in it. The search after the unattainable philosopher's stone has occasioned a thousand useful discoveries, which otherwise would never have been made.

But I must remind you, that it will be to very little purpose for you to frequent good company, if you do not conform to, and learn, their manners; fashion is tyrannical; the least revolt against it is punished by proscription. You must observe, and conform to all the *small* matters, if you will be in fashion yourself. Observe every word, look, and motion of those who are allowed to be the most accomplished persons. Observe their natural and careless air, their unembarrassed good-breeding.

Friendship

Take care to make as many personal friends, and as few personal enemies, as possible. I do not mean by personal friends, intimate and confidential friends, of which no one can hope to have half a dozen in the whole course of his life; but friends in the common meaning of the word, that is, people who speak well of you and who would rather do you good than harm, consistently with their own interest and no farther.

Be easy, and even forward, in making new acquaintances; but do not let your vanity make you suppose that people become your friends at first sight, or even upon short acquaintance. Real friendship is a slow grower, and never thrives unless engrafted upon a stock of known and reciprocal merit. Remember to make a great difference between companions and friends; for a very complaisant and agreeable companion may, and often does, prove a very improper and dangerous friend.

Suspect in general, those who affect any one virtue. They are commonly imposters, but not always so: I have sometimes known saints really religious, blusterers really brave, and prudes really chaste. Pry into the recesses of their hearts yourself, as far as you are able, and never implicitly adopt a character upon common fame.

There is an unrestrained friendship among young people, who are associated by their mutual pleasures only, which has, very frequently, bad consequences. Warm hearts and inexperienced heads, heated by convivial mirth and a little too much wine, vow eternal friendship to each other and indiscreetly pour out their

whole souls in common. These confidences are as indiscreetly repealed as they were made; for new pleasures and new places soon dissolve this ill-cemented connection; then ill uses are made of these rash confidences. Bear your part in young company. Trust them with your love-tales, if you please, but keep your serious views secret. Trust those only to some tried friend more experienced than yourself who, being in a different walk of life from you, is not likely to become your rival.

People will, in a great degree, form their opinion of you upon that which they have of your friends. A Spanish proverb says very justly, "Tell me whom you live with, and I will tell you who you are." One may fairly suppose that those who make knaves or fools their friends have something very bad to do or to conceal.

Marriage

Do not be in haste to marry, but look about you first, for the affair is important. There are but two objects in marriage, love or money. If you marry for love, you will certainly have some very happy days, and probably many very uneasy ones; if for money, you will have no happy days and probably no uneasy ones. In this latter case, let the partner at least be such a one that you can live decently and amicably with; otherwise it is a robbery. In either case, let them be of an unblemished and unsuspected character and of a rank not indecently below your own.

Self Improvement

I am very sure that anyone of common understanding may, by proper culture, care, attention and labor, make himself whatever he please, except a good poet.

People of sense never attempt impossibilities on one hand; on the other they are never discouraged by difficulties. In any point which prudence bids you pursue and which manifest utility attends, let difficulties only animate your industry. If one way has failed, try another; be active, persevere, and you will conquer. Content yourself with mediocrity in nothing.

Read people yourself, not in books but in nature. Adopt no system, but study them yourself. Observe their weaknesses, their passions, their humors. You will then know that they are to be gained, influenced or led, much oftener by little things than by great ones; and you will no longer think those things little which tend to such great purposes.

Swallow all your learning in the morning, but digest it in company in the evening. The reading of ten new characters is more than the reading of twenty old books. If you would be great in the world when you are old, shine in it while you are young; know everybody and endeavour to please everybody. Try

to engage the heart of every woman and the affection of almost every man you meet with.

Study the heart and mind of people, and begin with your own. The surest way to judge of others is to examine and analyse one's self thoroughly. Whatever engages or disgusts, pleases or offends you in others will engage, disgust, please or offend others in you.

Whenever you are with fashionable people with whom you are tolerably free, say frankly and naturally, "I wish ardently to please, but I have no experience of the world and do not know how to present myself. Have the goodness to show me your secrets of pleasing others." Never be ashamed nor afraid of asking questions, for if they lead to information, and if you accompany them with some excuse, you will never be reckoned an impertinent questioner.

Whenever you meet a person eminent in any way, feed him and feed upon him at the same time; it will not only improve you, but give you a reputation for knowledge and for loving it in others.

Read only useful books; and never quit a subject until you are thoroughly master of it, but read and inquire on til then.

Of all the troubles, do not decline, as many people do, that of thinking. The herd of mankind can hardly be said to think.

Education and Knowledge

Hoard up, while you can, a great stock of knowledge, for though, during your youth, you may not have occasion to spend it, yet a time will come when you will want it to maintain you.

Whatever knowledge you do not solidly lay the foundation of before you are eighteen, you will never be master of while you breathe. Knowledge is a comfortable and necessary retreat and shelter for us in an advanced age; if we do not plant it while young, it will give us no shade when we grow old.

Ignorant people are insignificant and contemptible; nobody cares for their company; they can just be said to live and that is all. The conversation of the ignorant is no conversation and gives even them no pleasure.

Observe the difference there is between minds cultivated and minds uncultivated, and you will, I am sure, think that you cannot take too many pains, nor employ too much of your time

in the culture of your own.

Books alone will never teach you; but they will suggest many things to your observation which might otherwise escape you; and your own observations upon mankind, when compared with those which you find in books, will help you to fix the true point. Deep learning is generally tainted with pedantry or at least unadorned by manners; as, on the other hand, polite manners and the turn of the world are too often unsupported by knowledge.

Abstain from learned ostentation. Speak the language of the company you are in. Speak it purely and unlarded with any other. Never seem wiser or more learned than the people you are with. Wear your learning, like your watch, in a private pocket, and do not pull it out merely to show that you have one.

Form a taste of painting, sculpture, and architecture, if you please, by a careful examination of the works of the best ancient and modern artists; those are liberal arts, and a real taste and knowledge of them becomes a fashionable person very well.

Spelling

I must tell you too, that orthography (spelling), in the true sense of the word, is absolutely necessary for a person of letters, or a gentleman or a lady. Reading with care will secure everybody from false spelling.

The Importance of Attention

One should always think of what one is about; when one is learning, one should not think of play; and when one is at play, one should not think of learning. If you do not mind your matter while you are at it, it will be a double trouble to you, for you must do it all over again.

A person without attention is not fit to live in the world. Without attention nothing is to be done: want of attention, which is really want of thought, is either folly or madness. You must not only have attention to everything, but a quickness of it, so as to observe at once all the people in the room, and yet without staring at them and seeming to be an observer.

Have attention even in the company of fools; for, though they are fools, they may perhaps drop or repeat something worth your knowing and which you may profit by. What is commonly called an absent person is commonly either a very weak or a very affected person; and, I am sure, a very disagreeable person in

company. However frivolous a company may be, still, while you are among them, do not show by your inattention that you think them so; but rather take their tone and conform in some degree to their weakness, instead of manifesting your contempt for them. That is the only way of doing it; for people will repay inattention with inattention, neglect with neglect, and ill manners with worse.

It is true that you will often be obliged to attend to things not worth anybody's attention; but it is a necessary sacrifice to be made to good manners in society. A minute attention is also necessary to time, place and character. An apt phrase in one company is not so in another, but, on the contrary, may prove offensive.

The Importance of Time

Very few people are good economists of their fortune, and still fewer of their time; and yet the latter is the most precious. There is time enough for everything in the course of the day, if you do but one thing at once; but there is not time enough in the year, if you will do two things at a time.

The steady and undissipated attention to one object is a sure mark of a superior genius; as hurry, hustle, and agitation are the never-failing symptoms of a weak and frivolous mind. Whoever is in a hurry shows that the thing he is about is too big for him. Haste and hurry are very different things. A person of sense may be in haste, but never in a hurry, because she knows that whatever she does in a hurry, she must necessarily do very ill.

Another thing, I must warn you against, is laziness. Pray be always in motion.

Method is the great advantage that lawyers have over other people. Lay down a method for everything and stick to it inviolably, as far as unexpected incidents may allow. Rise early

and at the same hour every morning, however late you may have sat up the night before. This secures you an hour or two of reading or reflection before the common interruptions of the morning begin; and it will save your constitution by forcing you to go to bed early, at least one night in three.

You will say that all this order and method is very troublesome, only fit for dull people. On the contrary; it will procure you both more time and more taste for your pleasures; after you have pursued it for a month, it would be troublesome to you to lay it aside.

I knew a gentleman who was so good a manager of his time that he would not even lose that small portion of it which the calls of nature obliged him to pass, but gradually went through all the Latin poets in these moments. He bought, for example, a common edition of Horace, of which he gradually tore off a couple of pages, carried them to that necessary-place, read them first, and then sent them down as a sacrifice to Cloacina; this was so much time fairly gained; I recommend you follow his example.

Business

As far as you can possibly, pay for everything you buy and avoid bills. Pay it yourself, too, and not through the hands of any other. When you must have bills, pay them regularly every month, and with your own hand. Never, from a mistaken economy, buy a thing you do not want because it is cheap. Keep an account in a book of all that you receive, and of all that you pay; for no one, who knows what he receives and what he pays, ever runs out.

How many people does one meet with everywhere, who with very moderate ability, and very little knowledge, push themselves pretty far, singly by being sanguine, enterprising and persevering? They will take no denial from man or woman; difficulties do not discourage them; repulsed twice or thrice, they rally, they charge again, and nine times in ten prevail at last.

In business nothing is more effectual, or successful, than a good, though concealed, opinion of one's self, a firm resolution, and an unwearied perseverance. None but madmen attempt impossibilities; and whatever is possible, is one way or another to be brought about. If one method fails, try another, and suit your methods to the characters you have to do with. Sense must distinguish between what is impossible, and what is only difficult; and spirit and perseverence will get the better of the latter. Everyone is to be had one way or another.

In business, how prevalent are the Graces, how detrimental is the want of them. Take this rule for granted, as a never-failing one; that you must never seem to affect the character in which you have a mind to shine. Modesty is the only sure bait when you angle for praise.

Never talk of business but to those with whom you are to transact it, and learn to seem vacuous and idle when you have the most business. You will negotiate with very little success, if you do not, previously, by your manners, conciliate and engage the affections of those with whom you are to negotiate.

The first thing necessary in writing letters of business is extreme clearness and perspicuity; every paragraph should be so clear and unambiguous, that the dullest person in the world may not be able to mistake it, nor obliged to read it twice in order to understand it. In business, an elegant simplicity, the result of care, not of labor, is required.

Business can never be done without method.